GAME CHANGERS

STORIES OF HIJABI ATHLETES FROM AROUND THE WORLD

CHARLENE SMITH

ILLUSTRATED BY
NATALYA TARIQ

ORCA BOOK PUBLISHERS

Published in Canada and the United States in 2025 by Orca Book Publishers.
orcabook.com

Library and Archives Canada Cataloguing in Publication
Title: Game changers : stories of hijabi athletes from around the world / Charlene Smith ; illustrated by Natalya Tariq.
Names: Smith, Charlene (Author of Game changers), author. | Tariq, Natalya, illustrator.
Description: Includes bibliographical references and index.
Identifiers: Canadiana (print) 20240358538 | Canadiana (ebook) 20240358546 |
ISBN 9781459838048 (hardcover) | ISBN 9781459838055 (PDF) | ISBN 9781459838062 (EPUB)
Subjects: LCSH: Muslim athletes—Biography—Juvenile literature. | LCSH: Women athletes—Biography—Juvenile literature. | LCSH: Muslim women—Biography—Juvenile literature. | LCSH: Hijab (Islamic clothing)—Juvenile literature. | LCGFT: Biographies.
Classification: LCC GV697.A1 S65 2025 | DDC j796.092/58297—dc23

Library of Congress Control Number: 2024936417

Summary: This illustrated nonfiction anthology features the stories of 13 inspiring hijabi athletes from around the world.

Orca Book Publishers is committed to reducing the consumption of nonrenewable resources in the production of our books. We make every effort to use materials that support a sustainable future.

Orca Book Publishers gratefully acknowledges the support for its publishing programs provided by the following agencies: the Government of Canada, the Canada Council for the Arts and the Province of British Columbia through the BC Arts Council and the Book Publishing Tax Credit.

Cover and interior artwork by Natalya Tariq.
Design by Troy Cunningham.
Edited by Kirstie Hudson.

Printed and bound in South Korea.

28   27   26   25 • 1   2   3   4

For Abubakr, Omar, Uthman, Khadija,
Ali, Abdullah, Iylah, Ameerah, Aamina,
Aarifa, Aabidah and Adeeba. I love you all.

And for Nagham Abu Samra, the Palestinian
champion and martyr who taught karate
to girls in Gaza because she wanted
every girl to feel her own strength.

CONTENTS

GAME CHANGERS

SPORT: Wrestling

LATIFAH MCBRYDE

PAGE 29

GAME CHANGERS

SPORT: Skateboarding

NADEEN ALHAMAD

PAGE 33

GAME CHANGERS

SPORT: Running

RAHAF KHATIB

PAGE 37

GAME CHANGERS

SPORT: Parkour

SARA MUDALLAL

PAGE 41

GAME CHANGERS

SPORT: Archery

REPRESENTS: Kenya

SHEHZANA ANWAR

PAGE 45

GAME CHANGERS

SPORT: Triathlon

REPRESENTS: Iran

SHIRIN GERAMI

PAGE 49

GAME CHANGERS

SPORT: Downhill mountain bike racing

REPRESENTS: England

SUMAYYAH GREEN

PAGE 53

Shehzana Anwar prepares to shoot an arrow at the 11th African Archery Championship in Namibia. This is the championship that earned her a spot at the Olympics.

Latifah McBryde defends during a wrestling match at the 2022 U20 Junior World Team Trials in Texas.

Fitriya Mohamed takes a shot on the basketball court—her home away from home.

Fatima Al Ali controls the puck during a game against the Dubai Gazelles.

FOREWORD
by SHIREEN AHMED

Throughout history we have learned about heroes in sports. We have listened to the tales of great athletes, brave competitors, kind teammates—people who show us what sportsmanship truly is. On social media we see videos of moments of victory and heartbreaking loss. Among these stories of athletes and coaches are people we might not hear about as often but who are no less important—athletes who are Muslim women.

These athletes have contributed, competed and participated at the highest levels and in many major tournaments around the world. They are sprinting down the sidelines of World Cup soccer matches, fighting for equal pay, working against systems of racism and drawing attention to important issues in the sports world. And those stories matter. Even if they don't win a world title or any medals at all, their experience and their wisdom matter.

ATHLETES AND ADVOCATES

There are so many misconceptions about Muslim women. People accuse them of being weak or submissive because their faith requires that they cover their hair. But hair coverings don't diminish their abilities. These women are strong, determined and carried by their faith, not hindered by it.

The women whose stories you will read in *Game Changers* have not only been athletes but also advocates. They fought against people who didn't believe in them and policies that sometimes kept them from the sport they loved. While their athletic talents are from God Almighty, they did not have leagues and systems or teams that welcomed them. Even in women's sports, many Muslim women fought for inclusion against people who made it harder for them to participate. Their dedication, confidence and conviction got them through. These women don't just demonstrate passion and skill; they teach others and set examples we can learn from.

RIGHT TO PLAY

In my years as a sports writer, I have learned that sports isn't just what happens *on* the field or court but also what happens *off* it. In telling the stories of Muslim women or others who may be misunderstood or excluded, we learn how to create better spaces in sports. We understand that sport is truly for everyone—it does not have gender or religious limits. We all have a right to play in safety, in peace and without discrimination. I hope these stories help you understand more about Muslim women in sports and the value of inclusive competition. May we all help to make the sports world better and create more welcoming spaces. Ameen.

INTRODUCTION

There are already books about women in sports and several that feature **Muslim** women. So why did I write a book about Muslim women in sports? And why did I include only women who wear the **hijab**?

I grew up in a non-Muslim family in Canada. I spent my childhood playing soccer, riding my bike, swimming and skating. In high school I competed in track and cross-country running. I converted to **Islam** when I was 19 and started wearing a hijab two weeks later. Suddenly, playing sports wasn't so simple. Would I overheat while running in all those clothes? Would I be allowed in a swimming pool with my hijab? What would the aunties from the mosque say about my running around outside? Was I even allowed to play sports as a Muslim woman? The answers to these questions were different depending on whom I asked.

AMAZING MUSLIM WOMEN

I decided it was easier and safer to avoid sports altogether if I wanted to be a good Muslim woman. But after my daughter was born, I realized that I wanted her to have the same opportunities I'd had as a child. I wanted her to be able to play sports and at the same time be able to wear a hijab if she chose to do so. So I did my own research and discovered many amazing Muslim women who wear the hijab and play all kinds of sports. And I didn't find any evidence that Islam forbids this. In fact, Islam encourages both men and women to be healthy and strong. The cultures of Muslim countries vary widely, and different cultures have different views on women playing sports in public. Even within the same culture, individual Muslims have different levels of comfort with this and different opinions on whether it is acceptable or not. This is one of many barriers that Muslim women must overcome as athletes.

HIJABI CHALLENGES AND SUCCESSES

Muslim women who wear the hijab while competing in sports face even more challenges than Muslim women who don't wear it. We stand out because we cover our heads and bodies, while our teammates and fellow athletes wear tank tops, short sleeves, shorts and swimsuits. We struggle to find clothing that is modest and technical enough for sports performance. We often face rules within our sports that do not allow us to cover our heads, arms and legs while competing and must push for rule changes to accommodate our needs. But the hijab is an important part of our religion. It is a symbol of our faith and obedience to God. So we wear the hijab proudly and don't let it stop us from doing what we love and reaching our goals.

During my research for this book, I interviewed the 13 athletes you will read about. It was so much fun to hear their stories firsthand and share them with you. I want to celebrate these women who have overcome challenges and have excelled in their sports, inspiring and encouraging people around the world.

CHASE YOUR DREAMS

In these pages you will read about amazing Muslim women who have fought for their rights and for the rights of all Muslim girls. You will learn about athletes who participate in well-known sports such as basketball and ice hockey, as well as athletes who participate in sports that aren't as well known, such as downhill mountain bike racing and parkour. You will meet women from Western countries, including the United States and Canada, and from Muslim-majority countries, such as the United Arab Emirates and Afghanistan. You will discover their struggles and celebrate their triumphs. And I hope you will be inspired to follow in their footsteps and chase your dreams.

Doaa Elghobashy sits in a volleyball heart, showing love for her sport!

DOAA ELGHOBASHY

Sumayyah Green takes off down the track at a World Cup race in Austria.

YASMEEN GREEN

THE FAMOUS PHOTO

DOAA ELGHOBASHY

SPORT: Beach volleyball
BORN IN: Beheira, Egypt

LIVES IN: Egypt
REPRESENTS: Egypt

One of the most *iconic* images from the 2016 Olympic Games in Rio de Janeiro is of Egyptian beach volleyball player Doaa Elghobashy coming face-to-face at the net with her German opponent, Kira Walkenhorst. What's so special about this photograph? While Kira is wearing a bikini, the standard uniform for female players, Doaa is wearing a long-sleeved shirt, full-length leggings and a headscarf. For many people, this image represents the mingling of cultures that is at the heart of the Olympic Games. For Doaa, it represents a major accomplishment.

Her father, a volleyball player himself, introduced her to the sport when she was eight years old, and it was a good match for Doaa's competitive nature. She began playing on an indoor volleyball team, which has six players on each team. As time went on, Doaa wanted more personal responsibility in her matches, so she switched to beach volleyball. In beach volleyball, each team consists of only two players, which gave Doaa the challenge she was looking for.

OPENING DOORS

Competing in the Olympics has always been Doaa's goal. When she started wearing the hijab at age 11, she knew that the standard uniform for female beach volleyball players was the bikini, and she knew that she would never wear one. She also knew she wasn't going to let that stop her. She intended to go to the Olympics with her hijab, no matter what anyone said.

Until recently beach volleyball players were only allowed to wear long sleeves and long pants during cold-weather matches. Before the 2012 Summer Olympics in London, the International Volleyball Federation (FIVB) changed the rules to allow more modest clothing options. This was great news for Doaa. When she and her teammate, Nada Meawad, competed in the 2016 Games, they made history as the first athletes to represent Egypt in Olympic beach volleyball, and Doaa made history as the first Olympic beach volleyball player to compete in a hijab.

After the famous photo went viral, Doaa became a celebrity in the Olympic Village. She was recognized everywhere she went. When she found out the reason for her newfound fame, she was thrilled. Even though her team wasn't a favorite to win a medal, their last match in Rio de Janeiro was played in front of a sold-out crowd of 10,000 fans. They were cheering for Doaa and chanting her country's name. People wanted to see and support the famous *hijabi* beach volleyball player.

Doaa says it was an amazing experience to play in front of that crowd and to be recognized for who she is and what she does. And it was inspiring for all the young Muslim girls around the world to see Doaa making history, knowing that she was opening doors for them to achieve their own goals.

HOCKEY HEROES

FATIMA AL ALI

SPORT: Ice hockey
BORN IN: Abu Dhabi, United Arab Emirates

LIVES IN: United Arab Emirates
REPRESENTS: United Arab Emirates

Fatima Al Ali had the experience of a lifetime when she met her hockey heroes and did the ceremonial puck drop at an NHL hockey game. This was a dream come true, and it all happened because of her amazing puck-handling skills. But there was a time when Fatima didn't know anything about hockey.

When she was growing up in the United Arab Emirates (UAE), there were no hockey games to watch on TV and no hockey leagues for Fatima to join. She discovered hockey thanks to a prize she got with a fried-chicken kids' meal when she was seven years old. The prize was a movie, and because she loved sports, Fatima chose *The Mighty Ducks*—a movie about kids playing hockey. She went home and watched it with her brother and her cousins, and she was hooked.

Fatima wanted to play hockey, but there were no hockey leagues for girls in the UAE, and as far as she knew, there was no hockey at all in her country.

"Keep on chasing your
dream, your goal, and
don't stop until you reach
your goal 'cause nothing
is impossible."

FATIMA
AL ALI

But there were skating rinks, so Fatima decided to teach herself to skate. At first she couldn't even stand up with her skates on, but her mom drove her to the local rink often, where she practiced until she was comfortable on the ice. When she wasn't at the rink, she was outside, skating on her inline skates. She kept her connection to hockey alive throughout her teenage years by skating and watching hockey movies.

GETTING HER CHANCE

One day, when she was 18, Fatima saw a brochure for a hockey tournament. She couldn't believe it—the UAE had a national hockey team after all! Fatima went to the tournament to watch the games and to take photos, which is one of her hobbies. On the second day of the tournament, she was asked to be the team's official photographer.

Fatima had held that job for two years when the UAE finally established a women's hockey team. She joined the team and held a hockey stick in her hands for the first time when she was 21. They competed internationally and improved a lot over the years, but Fatima wanted more. She also wanted to play on the men's team, but this was unheard of. They wouldn't accept her no matter how hard she worked or how well she played—until, that is, one day when she proved how tough she could be.

Fatima is a referee for the Emirates Hockey League (EHL), the top men's league in the UAE. When a fight broke out between players at a game she was refereeing, Fatima got in the middle of it and tried to break it up. Because she is much smaller than the male players, they didn't see her, and when she pushed one of them from behind, he turned and punched her in the face, not knowing it was her. Fatima left the ice to calm down and compose herself, and then she returned to finish her job. After they saw this, players from the Abu Dhabi Hockey League (ADHL) told her that she was welcome to play in their league. Since then she has been playing for both the men's and women's teams, coaching younger players and working as a referee. And she continues to achieve new goals. Fatima started playing hockey professionally in 2023, after being invited to join a women's team in Kazakhstan.

THE BEST THING THAT'S EVER HAPPENED

When former NHL player Peter Bondra was in the UAE, coaching at a hockey camp, he happened to see Fatima balancing a puck on her stick and flipping it back and forth quickly and with ease. He took a video that went viral after he posted it online. He then surprised Fatima with a trip to Washington, DC, which is where she met her favorite NHL team, the Washington Capitals. While in Washington, Fatima got to practice with the Capitals and impress them with her skills, watch the warm-ups from the bench and do the ceremonial puck drop. She says the trip was the best thing that's ever happened to her. She returned home with selfies and memories to last a lifetime.

FITRIYA MOHAMED

SPORT:
Basketball

BORN IN:
Herero, Ethiopia
LIVES IN: Canada

Fitriya Mohamed was born on Eid al-Fitr, the holiday marking the end of the holy month of *Ramadan.* She spent her childhood playing outside and watching her cousins' soccer games. She moved to Canada with her older sister when she was 10 years old. Her mom and her younger siblings had fled Ethiopia three years earlier because of the civil war happening in the country. Fitriya and her sister stayed behind with family while their mom got settled in Canada. After three years they were excited to finally be reunited.

When Fitriya started school in Toronto, she often felt left out because she didn't speak English. She couldn't understand what the teachers were trying to teach her, and she didn't have the words to ask for the help she needed. The one place where she felt she belonged was gym class. Language wasn't as important there, and she learned through watching and playing.

13

> **"Don't feel like you have to fit in with the rest of society. An original is better than a copy."**

FITRIYA MOHAMED

Basketball was Fitriya's favorite of all the new sports she was learning. She lived in a small apartment where she had to be quiet, but on the court she could run and make as much noise as she wanted.

TEAM PLAYER

In high school not many girls in her school played sports, so Fitriya played on every team that needed players. She started wearing the hijab when she arrived in Canada, which made her stand out, and on some teams she felt like she didn't belong. But when she played basketball, she never felt that way. Even though there weren't any other hijabis on her team, there were other girls of color, and all of her teammates accepted her as she was. She took basketball seriously and improved her skills by attending clinics and practicing whenever she could.

Fitriya was the first person in her family to attend university, and she wanted to focus on her studies and make her mother proud. But she still wanted to be involved in basketball, so she studied sport management and used her knowledge to encourage and support other Muslim girls and women to join her on the court.

MUSLIM WOMEN'S SUMMER BASKETBALL LEAGUE

In February 2020 Fitriya launched the Muslim Women's Summer Basketball League (MWSBL). Because of the COVID-19 pandemic, she wasn't able to offer any programs until the summer of 2022, when she finally launched the first season of MWSBL. It was a seven-week tournament-style league that welcomed Muslim girls and women aged 13 and older, as well as **allies**. Ninety girls and women registered, forming eight teams. Some of the participants had experience playing basketball, and some were trying it out for the first time. The league was a huge success. It also offered postseason basketball clinics so that those new to basketball could improve their skills. More programs are being offered as the league grows, and there are plans to create even more opportunities for girls and women in Toronto and even in other parts of the world.

Fitriya would like to travel to Ethiopia to develop basketball programming for the girls and women there, and possibly in other African countries as well. She has benefited so much from playing basketball, and she wants to share that with others. She wants girls and women everywhere to have opportunities to play sports and to experience the joy of being active and part of a team. She is on a mission to change the world through basketball, and she is just getting started.

HAJAR ABULFAZL

SPORT: Soccer

BORN IN:
Kabul, Afghanistan

LIVES IN: United States

REPRESENTS:
Afghanistan

From the time she was very young, Hajar Abulfazl heard people in her community say they felt sorry for her father because he had too many daughters. They asked what good it is to have so many girls when all they can grow up to do is stay at home and cook and clean. But Hajar's parents do not feel this way. They love and value all their children—four boys and nine girls. But such beliefs about girls were common in Afghanistan. Hajar was determined to change this and to make people see that girls can do more than stay at home.

When she was 14, Hajar started playing soccer on her school team. She decided that this would be the way she would try to change things—she would show the power of girls through soccer. Girls could be successful and strong. For the first year and a half, Hajar didn't tell anyone that she was playing soccer. But when her team entered the city tournament, she had to let her parents know. When she played at school, she just wore her school uniform. But for the tournament, she needed a proper soccer uniform, and she would have to ask her dad to buy it for her. She would also have to ask him for permission to play. Hajar was sure he would say no, but he surprised her. He took her by the hand, and they went to the sports shop to buy everything she needed.

OPPORTUNITIES AND OBSTACLES

Hajar's team finished second in the tournament, and there were scouts from the Afghanistan Football Federation watching. They chose Hajar and several other girls to play for their Kabul City team. Hajar was thrilled, but not everyone in her family felt the same way. Her mother's family was very conservative, and they didn't want Hajar to play soccer. One of her uncles told her that no one would ever marry her if she kept playing soccer. Another uncle would come to her house and try to stop her from going to games and practices. He told her that if she ever had sons, they would be ashamed of her. This upset Hajar, but she knew that she wasn't doing anything wrong. Her parents supported her, and her dad taught her that when you start something, you should finish it.

After playing on the Kabul City team for a year, Hajar was chosen for the Afghanistan women's national team in 2008. She played on that team for nearly 10 years and served as its co-captain. During this time Hajar was also pursuing a medical degree and working as the head of the women's committee for the Afghanistan Football Federation. It was her job to build trust between the girls' families and the federation. She visited families in their homes, trying to make them understand that it was good for girls to play soccer and that their daughters could play while still following their religion and respecting their culture. She also visited schools and brought photos of the national team to show the girls that the uniforms were appropriate, with long sleeves, pants and hijabs. It wasn't easy, but Hajar's hard work paid off, and during her years as the head of the women's committee, more than 5,000 girls registered to play soccer.

MISSION ACCOMPLISHED

In 2017 Hajar was invited to New York City to attend the Beyond Sport Global Awards. She was one of four people shortlisted for the Courageous Use of Sport Award, for individual bravery in the face of adversity. Hajar won the award, and the news spread throughout Afghanistan. Everyone was talking about it, including her very conservative family members. They called to congratulate her and tell her they were proud of her. The uncle who had told her that no one would marry her even called and said he would like her to marry his son. (It is acceptable in many countries, including Afghanistan, for cousins to marry each other.) She declined the offer.

Now, instead of people feeling sorry for her dad for having so many daughters, they congratulate him on his daughter's accomplishments.

KIANDRA BROWNE

SPORT:
Basketball

BORN IN:
Montreal, Canada
LIVES IN: United States

"Ashhadu an la ilaha illa **Allah** wa ashhadu anna Muhammad Rasool Allah. I bear witness that there is no God except for Allah and that Muhammad is the Messenger of Allah." With these words, Kiandra Browne became a Muslim, and her life changed forever.

Kiandra grew up in Montreal, where she started playing sports at a young age. Over the years she participated in track and field, judo, soccer, volleyball, flag football and hockey. But her first love was *ringette*, which she started playing when she was two years old. By the time she was in fifth grade, she was 6 feet 2 inches (188 centimeters) with her skates on. She was a physical player in addition to being tall, and she spent too much time in the penalty box. She was starting to question if ringette was the sport for her when she found out that it wasn't an Olympic sport, and that made her decision to switch sports an easy one.

> **"Fighting for something makes it better and makes it more beautiful."**

KIANDRA BROWNE

NEW BEGINNINGS

She was looking for a new sport, and with her height and family history, basketball was a natural choice. Her mother and grandmother were both basketball players, and she had always thought about playing basketball too. So she tried it, and she knew she had found her sport. She played for St. Laurent High School in Montreal, and her team regularly traveled to the United States, where she was noticed by college coaches and eventually recruited to play at the college level. She decided to play at Indiana University Bloomington, and that's where she was when she converted to Islam.

Kiandra grew up in a Christian family that didn't talk much about religion. Her high school at the time had a large Muslim population, and she had several Muslim friends. Through them she learned about Muslim prayer, the hijab and Ramadan. After high school, when she attended a Christian *prep school,* she'd asked her Bible studies teacher a lot of questions and hadn't been satisfied with the answers. While home from school, Kiandra caught up with some of her Muslim friends, who explained their beliefs. She was interested, so her friends took her to a mosque, where the *imam* gave her a copy of the Quran and some books about Islam. During the summer before her first year of college, Kiandra was inspired to pick up those books, and what she read about Islam felt natural and made sense. She took an Uber to the mosque, knocked on the door and converted. She was miles away from her family and her home, but she felt a sense of peace and belonging.

COMBINING BASKETBALL AND ISLAM

When she started her first year of university, her teammates didn't know she was a Muslim. But by the next year, she had started wearing the hijab. She was told she wasn't allowed to wear it covering her neck while she played that year but would have to wrap it around the front of her head and then tie it at the back, leaving her neck exposed. This made Kiandra uncomfortable. But she didn't get much support from the people around her and didn't feel like she should push the matter. When the season was over, Kiandra wrote an email to the *National Collegiate Athletic Association* (**NCAA**), telling them that she was going to wear her hijab covering her neck the next season. They didn't have a problem with that, and she was allowed to wear her hijab the way she wanted, which was good news for her and for her team. Kiandra is a valuable player, not only because of the points she scores on the court but because of the energy and enthusiasm she brings as well.

KULSOOM ABDULLAH

LIFTING WEIGHTS AND BARRIERS

SPORT:
Weightlifting

LIVES IN:
United States
REPRESENTED:
Pakistan

Kulsoom Abdullah never planned on entering a single weightlifting competition. And she certainly never planned on breaking down barriers and opening up the sport of weightlifting to Muslim women around the world. Kulsoom grew up in the 1980s. The only sports she saw women competing in on TV were track and field, figure skating and gymnastics. Her small town in the United States had limited sports facilities, and her parents were reluctant to leave her in the care of male instructors. So Kulsoom didn't participate in sports outside of gym class until she was in graduate school and decided to try taekwondo. When she wanted to gain strength for taekwondo, she started lifting weights. She couldn't have known how important weightlifting would become to her story and her life.

"Breaking barriers and defying norms isn't just about making a statement; it's about forging a path that empowers others to follow their own unique journey."

COMPETING

Her coaches encouraged her to enter a few local weightlifting competitions, and she enjoyed them. So she kept on competing, and one day she discovered that she had qualified to compete in a national competition. Up until this point, Kulsoom had been competing in the same clothes she trained in—long-sleeved shirt, exercise pants and a headscarf. This had never been a problem in local competitions, but her coaches told her that everyone who competes at the national level wears a *singlet.* The singlet leaves the weightlifter's arms and legs exposed so that the judges can see if competitors' knees and elbows are locked out (fully extended), which is required for a successful lift. Kulsoom couldn't wear a singlet and observe the hijab rules at the same time. She was the first hijabi weightlifter to reach this level of competition, as far as her coaches knew, and no one had ever asked for a religious *accommodation* to wear long sleeves and pants at a national competition.

When her coaches requested this accommodation from USA Weightlifting, it was denied. The Council on American-Islamic Relations (CAIR) put out a press release, which got a lot of attention in the news. USA Weightlifting invited Kulsoom to the next meeting of the International Weightlifting Federation (IWF). She gave a presentation to show the judges that they could still determine proper knee and elbow locks while her legs and arms were covered. Her presentation was a success, and the IWF decided to change its rule and allow Muslim women to compete while covered.

PAVING THE WAY

This rule change came after the national competition had passed, but it meant that Muslim women around the world who wear the hijab could start competing in weightlifting. Several countries in the Middle East now have female wrestlers competing at the national level because of this rule change. Sara Ahmed, a weightlifter from Egypt, made it all the way to the 2016 Summer Olympics, where she made history as the first Egyptian female athlete to win an Olympic medal. After the rule change, Kulsoom found out that Pakistan had a weightlifting federation and that only men competed. Because she held a national identity card for Pakistan and was able to get a passport, Kulsoom offered to compete for her parents' homeland, which she had visited throughout her life. She represented Pakistan at the Asian Weightlifting Championships as well as the World Weightlifting Championships, which encouraged other Pakistani women to join the sport. Pakistan was able to form a full women's team and now has women competing in both weightlifting and power-lifting, thanks to Kulsoom's efforts and example.

THE RIGHT TO WRESTLE

LATIFAH MCBRYDE

SPORT:
Wrestling

BORN IN: Buffalo, United States
LIVES IN: United States

Latifah McBryde and her sister Jamilah, both wearing hijabs and **abayas**, were standing in line to weigh in for a Brazilian jiu-jitsu tournament. Two other girls turned around, looked them up and down and said, "Oh, this is going to be easy." And it *was* easy—for Latifah and Jamilah. It never ends well for those who underestimate the McBryde sisters.

Latifah and her sisters all started wearing the hijab when they were four or five years old. They loved their hijabs and never let them stop them from doing what they wanted to do. The three youngest girls used to watch their brother wrestle, and one day the coach asked if seven-year-old Jamilah could join in the practice to wrestle with a girl who needed a partner. She had so much fun that her younger sisters, Latifah and Zaynah, decided they wanted to wrestle too.

The McBrydes were homeschooled, and wrestling was part of their physical education curriculum. Homeschooling gave Latifah the flexibility

> "If you're going to do something, do it all the way...put in the work and stay true to who you are."

to make her own schedule and include more training and wrestling classes in her daily routine. She didn't think she would ever be able to compete as a fully covered Muslim woman, but she always had a sliver of hope that one day maybe she would. With the support of their coach (their dad), Latifah and her sisters started to enter local jiu-jitsu and wrestling tournaments. People stared at them, wondering what these Muslim girls were doing at combat competitions. But they were allowed to wrestle, and no one seemed to mind that they were dressed differently—until they started to win.

ATTRACTING ATTENTION

In 2021 Latifah, Jamilah and Zaynah all competed at the US Women's National Championship and World Team Trials, in their respective age and weight categories. This was their first major tournament, and their dad got permission from USA Wrestling and United World Wrestling (UWW) for the girls to compete while wearing modest clothes. The competition went well, and there were no complaints about their clothing.

The next year Latifah and her sisters returned to compete in the 2022 US Women's Nationals and World Team Trials, and this time Latifah finished in second place. This meant that she qualified to represent the United States at the Pan American Games later that year. She was thrilled about the opportunity to represent her country at such a high level. Then her dad got a phone call letting him know that UWW would not allow Latifah to compete at the games unless she agreed to wear the standard wrestling singlet, which would leave her arms, legs and head exposed. Latifah would never agree to this.

Latifah and her father spoke on several podcasts, telling their story, and a petition was started, urging UWW to let Latifah compete while covered. In the end, she was not allowed, and the third-place finisher went instead.

MOVING FORWARD

All of Latifah's hard work and determination wasn't for nothing. After she placed second at the World Team Trials, Latifah was recruited by several universities. She accepted a scholarship from Life University in Georgia, which also offered scholarships to Jamilah and Zaynah. And because of the attention gained from the petition and the podcasts, the **National Association of Intercollegiate Athletics (NAIA)** and NCAA wrestling coaches got together and reviewed videos of the McBryde sisters' matches. They discussed whether or not modest clothing would be allowed in college wrestling, and all but one coach voted to allow it.

The coaches welcomed the McBrydes to their team and made them feel comfortable. The head coach even bought herself a hijab so that she could see what it was like to wrestle in one. In her first year on the team, Latifah was named Freshman of the Year and Wrestler of the Year for the entire Mid-South Conference. Latifah is a fighter, and she doesn't let anything keep her down.

NADEEN ALHAMAD

SPORT:
Skateboarding

BORN IN: Nablus, Palestine

LIVES IN: Palestine

In a skate park filled with mostly boys and men, Nadeen Alhamad practices her favorite trick, called a shuvit (or shove-it). While riding, she rotates the board as she hops up so that both feet leave the skateboard, and when she lands, the board has rotated 180 degrees beneath her feet.

When Nadeen was a kid, she played with her sisters and friends on the streets of Jenin. She was fascinated with inline skates, bicycles, skateboards...anything with wheels. She really wanted her own skateboard, but her mom wouldn't let her have one because she was afraid her daughter would get hurt. So Nadeen found other ways to have fun, but she never gave up on the idea of skateboarding.

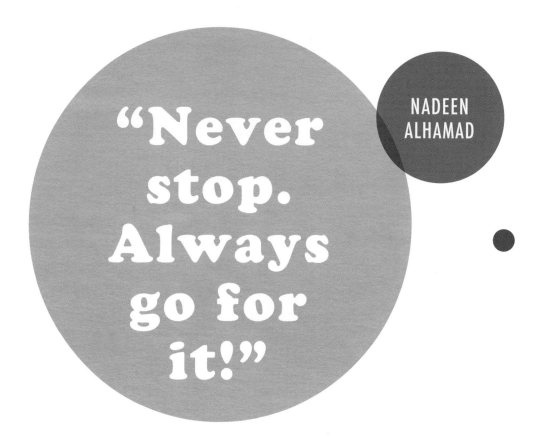

"Never stop. Always go for it!"

NADEEN ALHAMAD

GOING FOR IT

As a teenager, Nadeen watched videos of skateboarders, paying attention to how they moved and learning how to do tricks. When she started college, a friend told her that there was a skate park nearby. She started searching for skateboard shops, and she finally bought the skateboard she had always wanted with her own money and without telling her parents. She became a regular at the skate park, and everyone was very welcoming. Nadeen's parents were encouraging when they found out she had started skateboarding. Even though her mom still worries about her getting hurt, and always tells her to wear a helmet and safety gear, she is happy to see Nadeen doing something she has always wanted to do. Her mom even started taking her to the skate park, and sometimes Nadeen's sisters join her.

Nadeen met a young woman around her age at the skate park, and they became friends. She told Nadeen about a group she belonged to called Skater Uktis. It's a global network of Muslim women who skateboard, with members around the world. It offers online sessions on Islamic topics and in-person skate meetups and social events. The group provides community, connection and a safe space for Muslim women skateboarders. Nadeen joined Skater Uktis and is now their representative in Palestine.

In addition to her work with Skater Uktis, Nadeen is making a difference in her own family. Some of her young female cousins are interested in skateboarding, so she gave them her old skateboards so they could start learning. She shows them how to get up and keep going when they fall and how to be amazing skateboarders.

RUNNING TO REPRESENT

RAHAF KHATIB

SPORT:
Running

BORN IN:
Damascus, Syria
LIVES IN: United States

When Rahaf Khatib finally saw a hijabi athlete on the cover of a fitness magazine, she was elated. It was something she had prayed for and worked toward for a long time. There are few hijabi runners and many misconceptions about female Muslim athletes. When someone asked her if Muslim women are even allowed to run, it made Rahaf more determined than ever to show the world what Muslim women can do.

Rahaf left Syria when she was a year old. After taking her first steps on the airplane that brought her family from Syria to the United States, and running up and down the aisles while her dad chased her, Rahaf's love of running faded. In fact, she remembers skipping school when they had fitness testing just so she wouldn't have to run the mandatory 2 miles (3.2 kilometers).

RAHAF
KHATIB

"Never be afraid
to dream big...
whatever it is that
sets your heart
on fire, go
after it."

BECOMING A RUNNER

As a teenager, Rahaf hated sports, and as she grew into an adult, she still had no desire to be an athlete. When the students at her son's school were participating in a 1-mile (1.6-kilometer) run, one of the teachers told Rahaf that she should join in one of the longer races. Her first reaction was, "What? Me? No! I could never!" But then she decided that if everyone else could do it, so could she. After the race, she was exhilarated, and she wanted to do it again.

The following spring Rahaf ran her first half-marathon (13.1 miles/21.1 kilometers), and the next fall she completed her first full marathon (26.2 miles/42.2 kilometers). She went on to become the first Syrian to earn the Six Star Medal for completing all of the world's major marathons: Tokyo, Boston, London, Berlin, Chicago and New York City. This is an incredible achievement, especially for someone who used to hate running! Rahaf has now run more than 10 full marathons, over 35 half-marathons, two sprint triathlons and countless other races.

MORE THAN RUNNING

Even though running is an individual sport, Rahaf doesn't do it alone. Her parents, husband and children have always supported her. Her daughter participated in a running club for young girls that Rahaf coached, and her husband joined her in six of her marathons. She also raised over US$16,000 for Syrian refugees while running the Boston Marathon. This got a lot of attention from the media because it was during a time when **Islamophobia** was on the rise, and the so-called Muslim ban was in place, restricting travel to the United States from several Muslim-majority countries, including Syria. This made Rahaf even more determined to show Muslims in a good light and dispel myths and *stereotypes.*

When Rahaf entered a contest to appear on the cover of *Runner's World* magazine and was voted into the top ten out of thousands of contestants, she was the only finalist wearing a hijab. She felt like this was a sign from God that she needed to work hard to try to get more representation for Muslim women runners. She was then invited by another magazine to be included in its top ten female changemakers. And in October 2016 Rahaf appeared on the cover of *Women's Running* magazine. She finally got to see a hijabi on the cover of a fitness magazine—and the fact that she was that hijabi made the moment even sweeter.

SARA MUDALLAL

SPORT:
Parkour

BORN IN: Santa
Monica, United States
LIVES IN: United States

As Sara Mudallal let go of the cables, flew through the air and splashed down into the freezing-cold water, she was very wet and very cold, but she also felt blessed and honored. She was the first contestant to compete on the popular TV show *American Ninja Warrior* while wearing a hijab.

The show films at Universal Studios. Sara's episode was part of Jurassic World Night, so the atmosphere was especially exciting. But it was early spring, and the cool temperatures in Los Angeles at midnight, which is when the show was filmed, made the thought of falling into the water pretty daunting. Looking at the obstacles, Sara could tell they weren't ideal for smaller people like her, but she is all about getting past obstacles, and her goal that night was to at least make it past the first one.

The course started with a set of five floating pads, staggered on each side of a pool of water. Sara successfully leaped from pad to pad, and after

"I'm enjoying every minute of it!"

SARA MUDALLAL

jumping off the fifth one, she latched onto a rope dangling from above. She used the rope to propel herself to the steps that led to the next obstacle. She slipped and almost didn't make it across but managed to hold on and climb to the start of the second obstacle—the jumper cables.

Holding onto two cables hanging from the ceiling, Sara swung back and forth, building momentum, before letting go to try to latch onto the punching bag that dangled in front of her. She didn't make it and instead fell into the pool of icy-cold water below, while the crowd cheered her run. Even though she didn't win, just by being on the show Sara had succeeded in breaking stereotypes and motivating Muslim women to be active and to have fun—without changing how they look or who they are.

GETTING STARTED IN PARKOUR

Sara has been an athlete all her life. She started parkour when she was 20 years old—the same year she started wearing the hijab. In parkour, athletes try to get from one point to another as efficiently as possible, jumping, swinging, vaulting, rolling and doing whatever it takes to get past obstacles. The first time Sara went to a parkour gym, her dad went with her, and they both noticed there weren't many women at the gym. He was a bit worried about this, but Sara assured him that she would be fine. And she was more than fine. The people at the gym welcomed her with open arms, and Sara felt comfortable right away. Her first thought when she walked into the gym was, Wow! This is a huge jungle gym for adults! And as an adult who loves to play and move, Sara felt right at home. She was a natural, quickly learning many moves. Her favorite is one she calls the sidewinder. To do it, she places her right hand and left foot on the platform, then swings her right leg around while switching hands and pushing off the platform to land. She progressed through several skill levels quickly, becoming a recognized and respected athlete.

SHOWING THE WORLD WHAT SHE CAN DO

Sara started making videos of her parkour and rock-climbing feats and posting them on her Instagram and YouTube accounts. She has collaborated with popular *influencers* and has been featured on Fox News, Al Jazeera, CNN Sport and BBC. She participated in a competition in Utah and appeared in a video alongside Red Bull athletes. While traveling in her parents' home country, she collaborated with Red Bull Jordan to host a parkour event to bring athletes together and encourage girls to come out and try parkour. Sara wants to be the first hijabi in the stunt industry, and as a hero to so many Muslim girls already, she hopes to be cast as the first hijabi superhero in the Marvel Cinematic Universe.

SHEHZANA ANWAR

FROM ROBIN HOOD TO RIO

SPORT: Archery
BORN IN: Nairobi, Kenya

LIVES IN: Kenya
REPRESENTS: Kenya

Shehzana Anwar enjoyed watching *The New Adventures of Robin Hood* on TV as a child. After the show she and her siblings would go outside and cut down their mom's little trees to make their own bows and arrows. They had fun playing make-believe, but Shehzana never imagined she would still be shooting arrows as an adult. Years after those Robin Hood days, Shehzana and her family came across an archery display at a local outdoor exhibition, and they were encouraged to try it. They joined an archery club, and it became their regular weekend activity. It was a fun hobby, but Shehzana didn't take it very seriously. That changed after her first competition.

When she was 13 years old and had been practicing for a couple of years, Shehzana entered a local archery competition. Most of the other competitors were grown men who had many years of experience, so no one expected that Shehzana would beat them. But she did—all of them.

45

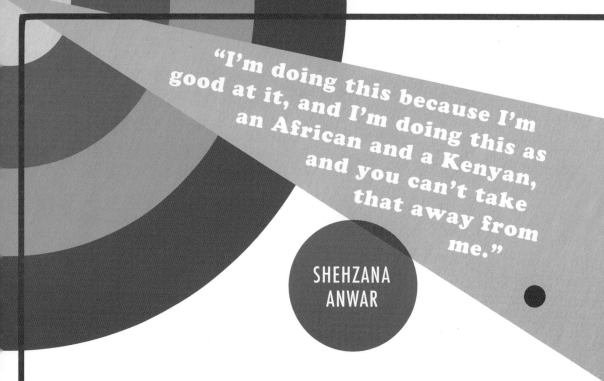

> "I'm doing this because I'm good at it, and I'm doing this as an African and a Kenyan, and you can't take that away from me."
>
> SHEHZANA ANWAR

For Shehzana, this victory was monumental. Growing up in Kenya, she'd seen that girls and boys were treated differently. Girls were expected to stay at home and cook and clean, while boys went out to have fun and do whatever they wanted. Doing better than all those men felt amazing. Shehzana got serious about the sport, and it became her life's work.

COMPETING AT A HIGHER LEVEL

Less than two years later, Shehzana had the opportunity to represent Kenya at the World Games in Germany. It was her first international competition. She traveled with her mother, who is her coach and is also now the national coach for Kenya. Because archery isn't popular in Kenya, a country known for its exceptional runners, archers have to pay for their own equipment, training and travel expenses. After the World Games, Shehzana went to other national and international competitions, and she and her family spent a lot of time and money on these trips. Whenever there was a championship to compete in, she was there, even when it meant having to delay her university exams.

Her biggest accomplishment, the one she is most proud of, is winning the African Archery Championship in 2016. This event is held every two years, and every four years the competition is also an Olympic qualifier. Shehzana worked hard to save up money for that trip, and when she won, it was all worth it—she had qualified to represent her country at the 2016 Summer Olympics in Rio de Janeiro.

THE OLYMPICS

Although she was eliminated from the competition early on, Shehzana had the experience of a lifetime at the Olympics. She competed along-side archers she had only ever watched online—celebrities in her world. Although Shehzana is proud to be from Kenya, she is often criticized because she is not the "right" color. She has fair skin because of her Indian heritage, and she says people often try to make her feel like she is not a true Kenyan because of this. Shehzana works hard to be the best at what she does, for herself and for her country, so she was honored to be chosen to carry Kenya's flag at the Rio Olympics opening ceremony. The flag was very heavy, and it made her think about the weight she had felt to prepare for the Olympics—the stress, the pressure and the responsibility of representing her country. She worried that the weight of the flag would tire her arms, which needed to be strong for the competition. But she knew she couldn't miss that amazing opportunity, and bearing the weight of the flag and the responsibility that came with it was all worthwhile.

SHIRIN GERAMI

SPORT: Triathlon
BORN IN:
Tehran, Iran

LIVES IN:
United Kingdom
REPRESENTS: Iran

Throughout her life, Shirin Gerami had heard people say, "Where there's a will, there's a way," and "There is no such thing as impossible." But she wondered if these statements were actually true or if they were just catchy slogans. She was about to find out.

Shirin was born in Tehran, Iran, but has lived in many different countries. When she was a student at Durham University near London, UK, she joined the triathlon club. When Shirin signed up for her first triathlon, she was pretty sure she wasn't going to finish. Triathlons have cut-off times for each of the disciplines. If someone takes too long in the swim or the bike or the run, they are disqualified from the race. Shirin decided she would just keep swimming until someone told her she was too slow. To her astonishment, that didn't happen. She was allowed to carry on to the bike portion and then the run, finishing the entire race. That day she learned to never give up without giving it her all.

> **"So many times we give up before even trying; before even starting the process, we decide that we can't do it and therefore never show up...at least start it and try it and give it what you have."**
>
> SHIRIN GERAMI

THE STRUGGLE

This lesson guided Shirin as she embarked on her unexpected journey to become Iran's first female triathlete. After university she joined her local triathlon club in London. It was 2013, and the International Triathlon Union (now World Triathlon) Championship was taking place in London that year. Her friends from the club were all talking about representing their home countries, and one of them jokingly asked Shirin if she was going to represent Iran. She laughed and said that wouldn't be possible.

Later that evening Shirin wondered why she had assumed it would be impossible. She found out that Iran had a triathlon federation. She emailed and asked if they would nominate her to represent Iran in the race. The federation responded as Shirin had expected—they did not support women competing in triathlons. But she didn't give up. She hoped that if she put in the work to get Iran's approval, other Iranian women would be given the same opportunities.

In Iran, all women are required by law to cover their bodies and hair, so even though Shirin didn't normally wear the hijab, she would have to if she was going to represent Iran. She needed clothes that complied with Iran's regulations and were also technical enough to allow her to perform at her best. The federation was willing to give Shirin a chance to find a solution, and she ended up with a custom outfit, designed in Iran, that met their requirements.

FINISHING STRONG

The night before the championship, Shirin still hadn't received the necessary written approval and nomination from Iranian officials. Less than 12 hours before the race was to begin, Shirin didn't know if she would be competing or watching from the sidelines. The written nomination arrived by email sometime during the night, and the next day Shirin became the first female triathlete to represent Iran, opening doors for all Iranian women.

She went on to compete at the Ironman World Championship in Kona, Hawaii, considered by many to be the hardest single-day race in the world. Shirin didn't need Iran's approval for this race, so she didn't have to cover her body and her hair. But she wanted to prove that choosing to cover does not make women less capable. The slogan she had seen on stickers plastered all over her home country—Your hijab is not a hindrance—was more than just a slogan. In the scorching Hawaiian heat, and fully covered, she completed the race in 13 hours and 11 minutes—well under the 17-hour cutoff.

DROPS, CRASHES AND FINISH LINES

SUMAYYAH GREEN

SPORT: Downhill mountain bike racing

BORN IN: London, England
LIVES IN: England
REPRESENTS: England

Sumayyah Green launched off the drop, soared through the air and crashed down onto the steep slope, heading into a *berm*. She had done everything right. She was mentally prepared, she knew the drop was coming, and she had followed her brother into the trail. But accidents happen, and in downhill mountain biking the consequences can be serious. As she landed, her handlebars snapped, and she ended up off her bike and on the ground. The other mountain bikers who saw her crash were worried about her, but Sumayyah walked away with only a fractured wrist and a broken bike, both of which could be repaired.

Downhill mountain bike racing is an extreme sport that involves riding at high speeds down steep, rough terrain that includes jumps, berms, drops and *rock gardens*. Sumayyah wears a full-face helmet, body armor, goggles

"If you want to do something you enjoy, do it! Don't hold back. It doesn't mean [that if] you wear hijab you can't do what you want. There are so many women out there doing amazing things."

SUMAYYAH GREEN

and gloves to keep her safe while she races. But no equipment can eliminate the risk of injury, so she has to be physically and mentally strong, and she has to stay focused to stay safe.

Sumayyah got involved in the sport when she was 13 years old. Her family had just moved from London to the English countryside, and her parents had decided that Sumayyah and her siblings would be **unschooled**. In addition to doing some math and reading every day, the siblings were expected to find something to focus on that they enjoyed. One of her older sisters took an online journalism course, one studied photography, and her brother took up downhill mountain biking. But Sumayyah couldn't think of anything that interested her. She spent a lot of time sitting around feeling bored until her dad suggested that she try downhill biking with her brother since she had enjoyed biking so much when she was younger.

BECOMING A RACER

Some of her happiest childhood memories were of biking with her family on the trails near their home in London. And she had always preferred the downhill sections to pedaling uphill, so Sumayyah agreed to give it a try. And she was happy that she did. Her dad got her a downhill bike, and she started racing.

Sumayyah has traveled to many exciting places for races, including Andorra, Austria, Croatia, Cyprus, Italy, Portugal, Scotland and Slovenia. And she never traveled alone. Along with her dad, and her brother who also competed, her older sister often came with her and worked as a professional sports photographer. Downhill mountain biking is a male-dominated sport, and Sumayyah and her sister were the only ones wearing hijabs at races. But that has never stopped her. Even when she was little, Sumayyah never hesitated to join in a soccer game at school, even if she was the only girl. And she and her sister have always felt welcomed and supported by the downhill mountain biking community. Sumayyah has competed in more than 50 races, including national and international championships and World Cup events. She loves the feeling of racing down the hill and the thrill of winning. She even loves her scars from all the times she has fallen.

MEET THE GAME CHANGERS

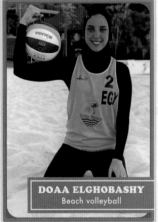

DOAA ELGHOBASHY
Beach volleyball

DOAA ELGHOBASHY

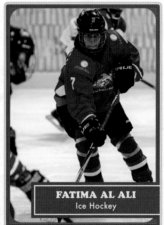

FATIMA AL ALI
Ice Hockey

MOHAMED ABDULHAMEED AL ALI

FITRIYA MOHAMED
Basketball

CHARLIE LINDSAY

HAJAR ABULFAZL
Soccer

ROY ROCHLIN/GETTY IMAGES

KIANDRA BROWNE
Basketball

INDIANA ATHLETICS

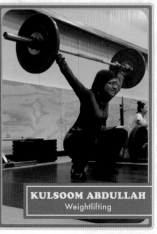

KULSOOM ABDULLAH
Weightlifting

KULSOOM ABDULLAH

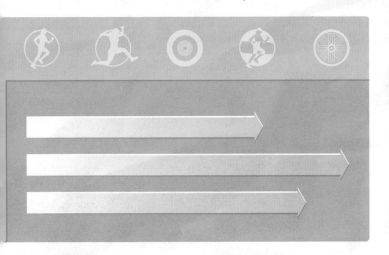

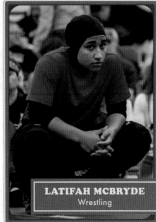

LATIFAH MCBRYDE
Wrestling

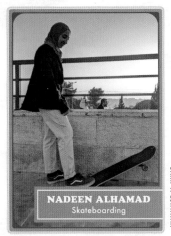

NADEEN ALHAMAD
Skateboarding

RAHAF KHATIB
Running

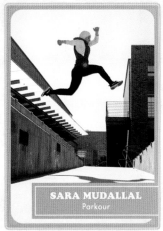

SARA MUDALLAL
Parkour

SHEHZANA ANWAR
Archery

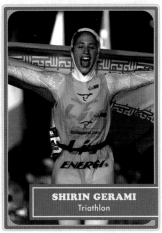

SHIRIN GERAMI
Triathlon

SUMAYYAH GREEN
Downhill mountain bike racing

MORE HIJABI ATHLETES

There are so many wonderful hijabi athletes, and they couldn't all be included in this book. Here is a list of more hijabi athletes from around the world.

ABTAHA MAQSOOD is a Scottish cricket player of Pakistani heritage who plays for Scotland's women's national cricket team.

AIFA AZMAN is a squash player from Malaysia who has won 11 Professional Squash Association titles and competes around the world.

AMIRAH SACKETT is an internationally acclaimed hip hop dancer, choreographer and dance teacher in the United States.

AMREEN KADWA is a rugby player from Canada. She is the founder and executive director of Hijabi Ballers.

ARIES SUSANTI RAHAYU is a speed climber from Indonesia who earned the nickname Spiderwoman when she broke the world record in women's speed climbing by reaching the top of the climbing wall at the 2019 International Federation of Sport Climbing World Cup in 6.995 seconds.

ASMAHAN MANSOUR was told she couldn't play with her team in the soccer tournament they had traveled to in Quebec unless she took off her hijab. She was 11 years old. She chose her hijab, and her team stood behind her, withdrawing from the tournament. She then spent seven years fighting against FIFA's no-headgear rule, until it was finally changed in 2014.

BATOULY CAMARA played basketball at the University of Kentucky and the University of Connecticut. She went on to play professionally in Spain and was a member of the Guinea women's basketball team. She founded WAKE (Women and Kids Empowerment), a nonprofit organization that empowers young girls through sport and education.

BILQIS ABDUL-QAADIR is a legendary basketball player who was a star on her high school and college teams. She was instrumental in having the International Basketball Association (FIBA) rule against head coverings changed in 2017.

FAIROUZ GABALLA started running in high school and also competed in martial arts. She continued her track-and-field career at the University of Prince Edward Island.

HEDAYA MALAK represented Egypt in both the 2016 and 2020 Summer Olympics and won a bronze medal in taekwondo each time.

IBTIHAJ MUHAMMAD was the first American Muslim woman to compete in the Olympics while wearing a hijab. She won a bronze medal in fencing in the team sabre event at the 2016 Olympic Games.

JAMAD FIIN played college basketball and served as captain of the Somali national women's basketball team. She competed in international FIBA tournaments, and she runs basketball camps for girls.

KHADIJAH DIGGS was the first hijabi to represent the United States in triathlon. She has also worked tirelessly to have appropriate triathlon suits available for hijabi triathletes, making the sport more accessible to Muslim women.

KHADIJAH MELLAH is a jockey in the United Kingdom. When she was 18 years old, she won the Magnolia Cup, a prestigious all-female *amateur* horse race. Khadijah was the youngest and least experienced jockey in the lineup and the first ever to compete while wearing a hijab.

KÜBRA DAĞLI is a taekwondo world champion from Turkey who, alongside her partner Emirhan Muran, won a gold medal at the 2016 World Taekwondo Championships.

MANAL ROSTOM, from Egypt, has run more than a dozen marathons and climbed several mountains, including Kilimanjaro and Mount Everest. She is the founder of the popular Facebook group Surviving Hijab and was instrumental in the development of the Nike hijab.

NAGHAM ABU SAMRA was a karate athlete in Palestine. She opened a club in Gaza to teach girls karate. She dreamed of representing Palestine internationally and establishing a national women's karate club. At age 24, she was killed during an Israeli airstrike.

NESRINE (NEZ) DALLY made history as the first hijabi Muay Thai athlete to compete in Thailand. She is also a coach and fitness instructor.

NOOR AHMED was one of the top junior golfers in Northern California when she graduated from high school. She earned scholarships to the University of Nebraska and became one of its top performers on the golf course.

NOOR ALEXANDRIA ABUKARAM was disqualified from a cross-country running meet in high school because she didn't have the proper waiver needed to run in her hijab. She helped write Senate Bill 288, which was passed in Ohio in 2020 and prohibits discriminatory policies in extracurricular activities.

NOR "PHOENIX" DIANA is the 2019 Malaysia Pro Wrestling Wrestlecon champion and the world's first hijabi pro wrestler.

NOUHAILA BENZINA is a Moroccan soccer player who made history at the 2023 Women's World Cup by being the first athlete to play while wearing a hijab.

RUMAYSA KHAN is a Canadian soccer player. She is the goalkeeper for Pakistan's national women's football team and for the University of Calgary Dinos.

RUQAYA AL-GHASRA is a sprinter from Bahrain. She represented her country at the 2004 and 2008 Olympic Games as well as the 2009 World Championships in Athletics. She has won multiple medals in continental games and championships.

SAFIYA AL-SAYEGH was the first rider from the United Arab Emirates to race in the Women's WorldTour and is the first Arab female professional cyclist.

TINA RAHIMI was the first-ever Muslim Australian woman boxer in the Commonwealth Games, where she won a bronze medal in 2022.

ZAHRA LARI was the first hijabi and the first Emirati to compete in figure skating internationally. She is a five-time Emirati national champion.

ZAHRA NEMATI became the first Iranian woman to win an Olympic or Paralympic gold medal at the Summer Paralympics in 2012. In 2016 she competed in archery in both the Olympics and Paralympics in Rio de Janeiro, where she served as Iran's flag bearer during the opening ceremony.

ZEINA NASSAR is a German boxer of Lebanese descent. She was instrumental in the International Boxing Association's decision to allow women to wear the hijab in international competitions.

NEVER GIVE UP

There are so many girls and women around the world who are chasing their dreams, reaching their goals and excelling in sports, all while proudly wearing their hijabs and holding fast to their beliefs. They are doing what they love while unapologetically being who they are. We can honor their hard work and courage by working hard and being brave. We can help by standing up for what is right and speaking up when we see people being left out or treated unfairly. We can follow the examples of these amazing hijabi athletes by following our dreams and never giving up. And we can change the status quo without changing ourselves. We can be game changers.

Kiandra Browne warms up before a game at Indiana University.

INDIANA ATHLETICS

Nadeen Alhamad has fun skateboarding with friends in Palestine.

BAKR Y. ESHTAYAH

WHY DO MUSLIM WOMEN WEAR THE HIJAB?

You may be wondering why Muslim women even wear the hijab if it leads to so many challenges. The command for Muslim women to wear the hijab comes from the Quran, which Muslims believe is the word of God. An important part of Islam is following the teachings of the Quran, and for women this includes wearing the hijab.

Wearing the hijab doesn't mean just covering the head. For a Muslim woman, wearing the hijab means covering her entire body except for her face, hands and sometimes her feet. (Did you know that Muslim men also have rules to follow about covering their bodies? Muslim men must cover their bodies from the belly button to the knees.)

Of course, Muslim women don't wear hijabs all the time. The hijab must be worn in the presence of men who are not close relations. The hijab doesn't have to be worn in front of husbands, brothers, fathers, sons, uncles, nephews, grandfathers, grandsons, stepfathers, stepsons, fathers-in-law or sons-in-law. Athletes are often competing in front of crowds of strangers, including men, which is why they wear their hijabs while competing.

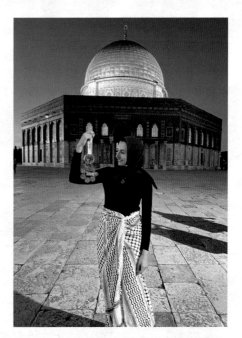

Rahaf Khatib holds up her medals in front of the Dome of the Rock in Jerusalem after completing a half marathon in Palestine in 2023.

RAHAF KHATIB

MODEST SPORTSWEAR

What does it take to make great sportswear for hijabi athletes? It varies from sport to sport, but most sportswear for any athlete, hijabi or not, will include some or all of the following qualities:

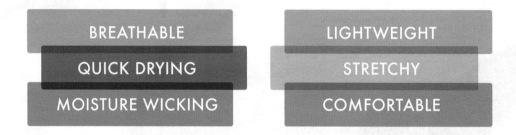

BREATHABLE

QUICK DRYING

MOISTURE WICKING

LIGHTWEIGHT

STRETCHY

COMFORTABLE

Hijabi athletes need clothing that meets the above requirements and is also appropriate Islamically. This means that their clothing must also have these qualities:

OPAQUE (NOT SEE-THROUGH)

NOT TOO TIGHT

COVERS THE ENTIRE BODY EXCEPT FOR THE FACE, HANDS AND FEET

Safety is also a concern when athletes compete while wearing the hijab. Hijabs used in sports shouldn't be closed with pins. They shouldn't have long ends hanging loosely or be wrapped in a way that is a choking hazard. There are many hijab styles available that are safe and comfortable for athletes. Now that you know the basics of modest sportswear for hijabi athletes, you can design your own!

GLOSSARY

ABAYAS—long, loose dresses with long sleeves

ACCOMMODATION—an adaptation or adjustment to something (like a rule) so that it better suits someone or meets a need

ALLAH—the Arabic word for God, used by Muslims, and by other people who speak Arabic

ALLIES—people who unite with, align with and help people of a certain group

AMATEUR—(adjective) involving athletes engaging in a sport without getting paid for it or as a pastime rather than as a profession

BERM—a banked corner found on mountain-bike trails

HIJAB—the Arabic word for veil/barrier, used to refer to the head covering worn by Muslim women

HIJABI—woman who wears a hijab

ICONIC—famous or popular; worthy of admiration or respect

IMAM—person who leads Muslim prayers

INFLUENCERS—people who have an impact on a large group of people who look up to them; usually refers to people with a large following on social media

ISLAM—the Arabic word for "submission." A religion whose followers believe that there is only one God (Allah) and that Muhammad is the Messenger of God.

ISLAMOPHOBIA—fear, hatred or prejudice toward Islam and Muslims

MUSLIM—the Arabic word for "one who submits." Someone who follows the religion of Islam.

NATIONAL ASSOCIATION OF INTERCOLLEGIATE ATHLETICS (NAIA)—the governing body for smaller college athletic programs in the United States

NATIONAL COLLEGIATE ATHLETIC ASSOCIATION (NCAA)—a member-led organization that regulates college and university athletic programs in the United States

PREP SCHOOL—short for college-preparatory school, a school that prepares students for college or university

RAMADAN—the ninth month of the Islamic calendar. Muslims fast (don't eat or drink anything at all) from dawn to sunset for the entire month of Ramadan.

RINGETTE—a team sport played on ice. Players skate while holding a straight stick, which they use to try to get a ring into the opponent's net.

ROCK GARDENS—sections of a mountain-bike trail that are covered with rocks

SINGLET—in wrestling and weight-lifting, a tight-fitting one-piece sport uniform that is sleeveless and ends above the knees

STEREOTYPES—general, over-simplified, commonly held beliefs about a group of people

UNSCHOOLED—a popular home-schooling method that allows children to learn at their own pace and focus on what they want to learn, without following a set curriculum

RESOURCES

PRINT

Abdul-Qaadir, Bilqis, and Judith Henderson. *Lion on the Inside: How One Girl Changed Basketball.* Kids Can Press, 2023.

Dabiri, Hafsah. *Basirah the Basketballer says Insha'Allah.* Ruqaya's Bookshelf, 2019.

Lari, Zahra, and Hadley Davis. *Not Yet: The Story of an Unstoppable Skater.* Orchard Books, 2024.

Maddox, Jake. *Running Overload* (A Jake Maddox Graphic Novel). Stone Arch Books, 2020.

Muhammad, Ibtihaj. *Proud: Living My American Dream* (Young Readers Edition). Little, Brown Books for Young Readers, 2019.

ONLINE

Crescent Sports Club: crescentsportsclub.org

Hijabi Ballers: hijabiballers.com

Islamic Games: islamic-games.com

Les Hijabeuses: Instagram: @leshijabeuses

MISS (Muslimah in Sport Society): Instagram: @muslimahinsport

Muslim Runners: Instagram: @muslim.runners

Muslim Sports Foundation: muslimsportsfoundation.org.uk

Muslim Women in Sport Network: mwisn.org

Muslim Women's Sport Foundation: mwsf.org.uk

Muslimah Athletic Association: maasports.ca

Muslimah Athletic Club: Instagram: @muslimahathleticclub

Muslimahs Endure: muslimahsendure.org

MWSBL (Muslim Women's Summer Basketball League): mwsbl.com

Sisterhood Softball: sisterhoodsoftball.com

Skater Uktis: skateruktis.com

ACKNOWLEDGMENTS

Thanks, above all, to The One who created the Heavens and the Earth and makes all things possible.

Thank you to my husband for always supporting me in every way; to my children for encouraging me to write a book and for being my biggest cheerleaders; to my mom and my sister for always being there for me and loving me unconditionally; to my mother-in-law for always helping me; to my editor Kirstie Hudson, editorial assistant Georgia Bradburne and the entire team at Orca; to my wonderful agent, Hilary McMahon, for believing in me and my book; to my sister in Islam and in agency, Rahma Rodaah, for everything you've done and continue to do for me; to Shireen Ahmed for writing the foreword, for being my expert reader and for all of your support and help with this book; to Natalya Tariq, for illustrating this book so beautifully; to all of my early readers who read drafts and provided feedback, especially Muna Abougoush, who was there for me every step of the way; to Na'ima B. Robert for making me feel like I could write this book; to Fiona Kenshole for your invaluable help and encouragement; to Nurshireen Abdul Rasid for helping me with translations; and last but not least, to all the athletes for sharing your amazing stories with me and the world.

INDEX

Page numbers in **BOLD** indicate an image caption.

BENJAMIN DENNIS

CHARLENE SMITH

is a hijabi who tries to keep up with her six children in various sports. She lives in Edmonton, Alberta, and spends her summers downhill mountain biking in the Coast and Columbia Mountains of British Columbia. *Game Changers* is her first book.

The author at Whistler Mountain Bike Park.

NATALYA TARIQ
is an illustrator based in Ottawa, who grew up in Russia and lived in Saudi Arabia. With a professional background in translation, Natalya has a keen interest in different countries, languages and cultures. She started illustration in 2021 as a hobby and developed her art into a second career.